ghetto sutras
remaining in the light

VOLUME I

THE CONSCIOUSNESS
OF TRANSCENDING SUFFERING
& RACISM

By Professor K. A. Shakoor, MAOM
(Israafiiyl El Ishvara Karma Minjur Tarpa)
Jannah Press

DEDICATION

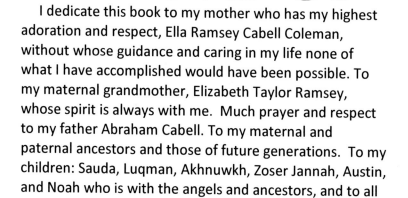

I dedicate this book to my mother who has my highest adoration and respect, Ella Ramsey Cabell Coleman, without whose guidance and caring in my life none of what I have accomplished would have been possible. To my maternal grandmother, Elizabeth Taylor Ramsey, whose spirit is always with me. Much prayer and respect to my father Abraham Cabell. To my maternal and paternal ancestors and those of future generations. To my children: Sauda, Luqman, Akhnuwkh, Zoser Jannah, Austin, and Noah who is with the angels and ancestors, and to all my grandchildren. To my teachers and my students past, present, and future, to all of humanity.

I pray that all suffering ends.

TABLE OF CONTENTS

ACKNOWLEDGEMENTS I

FOREWORD III

PREFACE VII

SECTION 1: TRANSCENDING SUFFERING 1

   Shamata 6

   Seven positions of Shamata: 9

   Tilopa's Six Words of Advice: 11

   Cobra Breath 13

   Clear Light Meditation 17

   QUESTION & ANSWER 20

SECTION 2: CAUSE OF SUFFERING:
            BUDDHISM AS A SOLUTION 23

   Suffering 25

   The Four Noble Truths: 29

   The Noble Eightfold Path 30

   The Three Jewels: 30

   QUESTION & ANSWER 33

SECTION 3: TRANSCENDING SUFFERING:
            MIND-BODY CONNECTION 35

   Spiritual Technology 37

     Figure 1: Primordial Sounds and Wisdom 39

     Figure 2: Five Buddha Families 39

   The Main Meridian Channels of Chinese Medicine 40

   QUESTION & ANSWER 41

SECTION 4: THE WORLD IS A GHETTO 45

   The Aim of Meditation 47

   My Mandala of World Peace 50

   QUESTION & ANSWER 51

CONCLUSION 57

GLOSSARY 59

RECOMMENDED READING 74

BIOGRAPHY 78

ACKNOWLEDGEMENTS

I would like to express my deep heartfelt thanks to Laurie Reisman, J. Carlo Diaz, Bridget Hardman, Jessica Miller, the staff at Xerograghics: Eric, Caroline, and James for all your hard work with the technical aspects of editing, transcribing, typesetting and creating images for this book.

I also acknowledge the heartfelt support and encouragement received from the Sangha at Karma Thegsum Choling Tibetan Buddhist Meditation Center, especially Lama Losang (Dr. David Bole, AP, Ph.D.) and Jessica Miller (Director.) My life long heart-soul brothers and sisters on the path: Aaron Eggelston, Prof. Karim Darwish, Hamid Drake, Anthony Lorenzo, Chris and Dan Murphy, Dhumrakesha Radha, Gloeane Steiger, Jennifer George, Rashid Abdullah, and Amina Saboor. My spiritual family in Philadelphia: sister Godis Shani Asantewaa, The Urban Shaman-Baba Ainowashi, my brother Baba Donald Perry "the Bishop" and Minister Enoch Tehuti Amen Ra-El at the ESP Tribal Foundation. Ruth Morrison and the staff and students at Dragon Rises College of Oriental Medicine, Community Education at Santa Fe Community College, Lilli at the Unified Training Center, Rona at Hip Moves.

Much respect and adoration for the Maahaah-Rooh current teaching instructors: David Peoples, Harry Lewis, Bruce Shaw, J. Carlo Diaz, Michele Bowers, Metin Ebcioglu, Lisa Marie Adams and Donald Perry.

My extended thanks and heart blessings to Laurie Reisman, J. Carlo Diaz, Bridget Hardman, Jessica Miller, Lama Losang, Ken Warren, Metin Ebcioglu and Lisa Marie Adams for your heartfelt support.

To all my teachers past and present: I send my deepest gratitude for all that you have given me. (See Biography)

I

ACKNOWLEDGEMENTS

FOREWORD

"The small man
builds cages for everyone
He
Knows.
While the sage,
Who has to duck his head
When the moon is low,
Keeps dropping keys all night long
For the
Beautiful
Rowdy
Prisoners"

This poem by Hafiz succinctly captures the essence of Ghetto Sutras. Shakoor compassionately engages the beautiful rowdy prisoners in all of us and empowers us with the keys for release. The contribution that Shakoor offers the reader through Ghetto Sutras is essential during a time period when humans are grappling with the fundamental issues of racism, classism, capitalism, sexism, and greed. I speak as a survivor of incest, rape, neglect and abuse and have been a part of the Personal growth movement since the early 1990's. It was after many years of giving myself the gift of being with and releasing my pain and cultivating my ability to listen to and hold space for others to share and release their pain that I was able to start to see my value as a human. I then found myself rising up to the systemic degradation that created a system that was built on the backs of beautiful indigenous beings. I soon became a Feminist and Prison Abolitionist. My activist and personal growth paths seemed to be divergent. I felt that something fundamental was missing and had a yearning for something deeper that would bridge the gap between the two. After being raped by one of my closest friends, I watched my beloved activist community fall apart. I found myself in an existential crisis and continued on my journey of self-realization. I found myself catapulted on a spiritual journey in which I quickly learned that my outer world is a mirror of my inner world. I learned that if I did not heal from how I was hurt as a young person, that I was likely to keep manifesting situations in my life that would allow me to relive the pain in an effort to heal. Utilizing Therapy, Re-evaluation Counseling, Personal Growth Seminars, Buddhism, Judaism and Vedic Teachings, I came to the understanding that everything that happened to me was a gift from higher powers in an effort to assist me to heal and to become closer to the Divine. I learned that capitalism is based on the myth of scarcity and pits humans against each other; however, if we don't heal our hurts, anything that we build to replace it may be just as corrupt. I saw that our suffering may cause us to do the work for the oppressive system. If we are busy fighting with each other than we are likely to be too distracted to build the type of world in which we want to live in. I learned that the time that we take spending on illusions (TV, material gain etc.) while stuck in our pain is immense and if we spend that same amount of time engaging in healing practices, we will see a floodgate of time open up in our lives that we didn't previously conceive of. Through several mystical experiences, I learned that I am not my body. This body is a vehicle that carries me through this lifetime to learn and to grow. It was when I started connecting to my higher self that I was able to see the synchronicity and beauty of life. Relationships began to heal and miracles began to unfold.

Ghetto Sutras is the vital perspective needed in today's tumultuous times that interweaves the perspectives of taking responsibility for clearing and healing our mind and hearts while also acknowledging the complex external systemic forces that hold humanity back from living our true potential. I met Shakoor at a local alternative library/reading room called the Civic Media Center in Gainesville, FL. He was showing the community a movie called Power to the People and shared with the group that the People's Movement of the 60's and the Black Panthers utilized Asian Medicine (Acupuncture) clinics in urban areas throughout the United States to assist healing in impoverished communities. I later saw Shakoor following suit at local Health and Wellness Fairs in which he presented energetic and Asian healing principles to veterans, homeless people and the community at large. I noticed right away that he is extremely talented at taking complex tools that have been historically difficult for the average person to obtain and simplifying them and making them accessible to the masses. Ghetto Sutras does just this. Shakoor filters through 50+ years of personal work and study with many Spiritual Masters and gives us the gems at the top of the sieve . He is generous, concise and potent with his knowledge. There is no honor greater than to be associated with a human whose purpose and endeavor in life are to assist humanity to reach their true potential. In the past year, I have had the blessing to attend Shakoor's Energetic and Meditation classes at the Gainesville Karma Thegsum Choling Tibetan Buddhist Meditation Center. My experiences in the classes have ranged from a deep sense of calm and peace to feelings of rebirth and renewal due to engaging in the practices that are outlined in Ghetto Sutras. In every interaction that I

have had with him, he endeavors to lift up, motivate and inspire those around him to live their life purpose. In Shakoor's presence, I experience the constant gift of freedom to be who I am without judgment or shame. Shakoor truly lives what he teaches, "Just be whatever you are in that moment and it dissolves itself. If you're happy, be happy. If you're sad, be sad. Totally embrace that sadness. If you're angry, totally embrace that anger. You don't have to do anything but embrace the feeling and eventually it will go away. That is the essence of Shamata."
- Ghetto Sutras

Immense knowledge and generosity pour through the pages of Ghetto Sutras. Ghetto Sutras empowers the reader with such precious jewels that when utilized, can take the reader towards liberation and freedom. Shakoor is a humble presence, therefore never taking personal credit for the brilliance that transforms around him. He continually gives credit and refers to his teachers. He continues to grow personally and spiritually and though I view him as a master, he is always ready to learn something new. Presently, he is a student of Lama Losang (Dr. David Bole, AP, and Ph.D.) who is the resident Lama at the Gainesville Karma Thegsum Choling.

Reverend Laurie Reisman, MSW, LCSW
Karma Dechen Palmo-Hochma Vida

PREFACE

The purpose of the Ghetto Sutras is to share the concepts of Universal Buddhism with people who are new to Buddhism or have had limited exposure. In the Western world, supporters of Buddhism have been largely middle and upper class. The material has been presented in such a highly academic format that it often alienates the majority of people. Our world is in dire need of a system that can truly address the sufferings of our time. This book is an attempt to present core Universal Buddhist Teachings in a society that is largely influenced by Christian, Jewish, Vedic and Islamic systems.

"He counseled that it is not helpful for one person to try and force their beliefs on another. This creates conflict, and harmonious relationships are very important. If we seek commonalities and a shared happiness, then change can happen. Sometimes we are too attached to our own religion. Of course, these traditions are important, but their goal of happiness and harmony is the most important." - His Holiness Gyalwang 17th Karmapa

Ghetto Sutras has several themes. Theme one is to present practices where one can control the mind, the breath, and be able to re-channel the primal energy (sexual energy). These serve as the foundation for attaining enlightenment.

The second theme is to show how racism has had such an effect on the world's suffering which is rooted in fear, envy, and greed. Ghetto Sutras points out the reality that energetic colors exist inside each human being. According to Asiatic medical systems, the color white represents the lungs and large intestine, red represents the heart and small intestine, yellow represents the spleen and stomach, and black represents the kidney and bladder and blue represents the liver and gall bladder which are connected to transcendental consciousness. In short, in order to be whole, human beings must transcend the mental attachment to color. To do otherwise is to stagnate our own spiritual progress and evolution.

The third theme of Ghetto Sutras refers the Buddha principle or the concept that we are already awake. It is our impure thinking that clouds the light (consciousness). What blocks this light is that human beings are over consumed with desire for materialism (impermanence), which is another cause of suffering. Buddhism states that a person should focus on the inner self (the mind), rather than on external manifestations. Buddha said, believe only in those things of which you have direct experience. This book is designed to assist one in cultivating a direct experience that will assist you to get in touch with your inner Buddha (inner revelations and realizations). In other words, this book is my truth and written from my experience, and my hope is that you the reader will discover your own inner light, path, and truth.

NOTE: The views expressed in this book might not necessarily follow the views of the Karma Kagyu, other Tibetan, or Asian Buddhist schools. This book is based on my personal revelations, studies, practice and realizations over fifty-two years.

NOTE: I have carefully selected a number of books and listed them at the end. These are spiritual and self-developmental books from a variety of traditions and philosophies. I highly recommend the reading of these to hopefully aid you in your evolutionary growth.

"Don't you know that It's true that for me and for you the world is a ghetto" – War, 1972

Revelation 18:1-8

1 - And after these things I saw another angel come down from heaven, having great power; and the earth was lightened with his glory.

2 - And he cried mightily with a strong voice, saying, Babylon the great is fallen, is fallen, and is become the habitation of devils, and the hold of every foul spirit, and a cage of every unclean and hateful bird.

3 - For all nations have drunk of the wine of the wrath of her fornication, and the kings of the earth have committed fornication with her, and the merchants of the earth are waxed rich through the abundance of her delicacies.

4 - And I heard another voice from heaven, saying, Come out of her, my people, that ye be not partakers of her sins, and that ye receive not of her plagues.

5 - For her sins have reached unto heaven, and God hath remembered her iniquities.

6 - Reward her even as she rewarded you, and double unto her double according to her works: in the cup which she hath filled fill to her double.

7 - How much she hath glorified herself, and lived deliciously, so much torment and sorrow give her: for she saith in her heart, I sit a queen, and am no widow, and shall see no sorrow.

8 - Therefore shall her plagues come in one day, death, and mourning, and famine; and she shall be utterly burned with fire: for strong is the Lord God who judgeth her.

"Don't you know that It's true that for me and for you the world is a ghetto" – War, 1972

PREFACE

SECTION 1

TRANSCENDING SUFFERING

There are many approaches to transcending suffering stemming from many cultures and spiritual traditions throughout the world. In this beginning theory and practice, the *method* and *means of transcending suffering* will be discussed before discussing the root causes. The following subjects discussed are a synthesis of what I

have been taught directly, my own personal experiences, study, and research through a lifetime journey in the spiritual sciences.

Yoga is the foundation of all of the major religions that are present today. It was invented by the ancients to help harmonize the mind, body, and spirit of mankind. For generations, this science was highly perfected by many great rishis, sages, or *Mahasiddhas* and passed down from teacher to disciple over thousands of years.

These spiritual technologies or practices that are the foundational steps to achieving this goal will be covered in this book, such as the practice of *Shamata* or Mindfulness, Cobra

Breath, and Clear Light Meditation. These three essential practices mark the beginning of a journey towards liberation (freedom) from the emotional, mental and spiritual suffering of a human being.

Buddhism is an ancient science that goes back millennia. From my research this spiritual science and technology, comes from the Ancient Tamil during the Dravidian cultures of Southern India. It is stated that the majority of original religions have their origin in ancient India of the Tamil and Dravidian Civilizations. This includes; Vedic, Buddhism, Jainism, Sikhism, Judaism, Christianity and Islam. India even has the physical shape of a heart, which is said to be the heart of the world and the central network which are the foundation of all spiritual traditions.

"All beings are confused and produce their future karma, falling into the ocean of life and death. They are trying to escape it; instead they fall back into it. Why? Because the self-nature was not yet seen."
- The Buddha

"All beings are confused and produce their future karma, falling into the ocean of life and death. They are trying to escape it; instead they fall back into it. Why? Because the self-nature was not yet seen."
- The Buddha

"Free your mind and your ass will follow. The
kingdom of heaven is within."
– Funkadelic (George Clinton)

Shamata

Shamata means "Mindfulness." It is a calm abiding practice
in the Buddhist tradition meant to tame one's mind. In

"Free your mind and your ass will follow. The kingdom of heaven is within."
– Funkadelic (George Clinton)

everyday life, we are bombarded with an excessive amount of mental stimulation through electronics such as television, cell phones, and computers. This can be overwhelming to the mind in a fast-paced society where one may have a job, a marriage and a family to support. The overabundance of mental stimulus becomes taxing on the mind resulting on one being "mentally drained." This creates a situation in which we are not able to concentrate or think clearly. This leads to emotional and mental imbalances.

Simply put, the nature of the mind is akin to water. It is very receptive and absorptive and can flow in the direction it is guided. Because of this, the mind being like water can be contaminated and become dirty over time. The mental "dirt" we accumulate in our minds begins to build to such a point that we have no control over our minds and we are seemingly stuck and unable to free ourselves. Another way of looking at it is that the dirtier the water of our minds becomes, the less we are able to perceive clearly what is going on around us. We, therefore, become confused and emotionally struggle throughout daily life. By practicing Shamata, we can consciously work on cleansing the muddied waters of our minds and empower ourselves so we no longer are victims to external stimuli. Instead, we can put our efforts towards achieving total balance, health, and happiness.

Below are the seven positions that one can follow to aid this process.

Seven Positions of Shamata

1) Choose a *sattva* or posture:

Assume one of the postures displayed in the figure below. Pick one that is most comfortable to you such as the sitting lotus posture or sitting on the edge of a chair or on the edge of your bed. Lying down should be avoided.

2) Keeping body erect and back straight

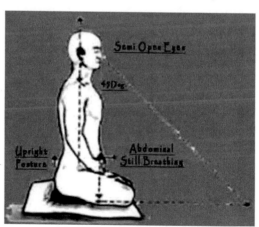

By straightening the spine, this allows the spiritual energies to align. (If this is uncomfortable at first it will strengthen the back muscles and in time it will get easier.)

3) **Thumbs touching the base joint of the ring fingers**
Fold the four fingers over the thumb and rest both hands face down on your thighs or knees. This is a *mudra* or hand posture meant to retain the "wind" which aids in taming the mind. (see glossary for definition of mudra and wind).

4) **Tucking in the buttocks and tightening the anal sphincter**
By tucking in the buttocks, this helps align the spine and by tightening the anal sphincter, this encourages spiritual energies to activate.

5) **Gaze the eyes toward the tip of the nose**
Gaze the eyes at a 45-degree angle about one arm's length in front of you. By gazing slightly downwards, this works on mind-clearing.

6) **Tongue at the roof of the mouth**
By touching the tongue to the roof of the mouth, this helps align energies between the mind and heart. When the heart is clear, so is the mind. When the mind is cleared, the heart is clear. The connection between the heart and the mind creates inward harmony.

7) **Pull the chin back (slightly tucked in)**
Pull the chin back slightly, further aiding the alignment of spiritual energies in the spine.

When you have accomplished all seven positions, you are now ready to begin Shamata. While holding the seven positions, then make an effort not to engage with any thoughts or images that may arise and simply be the witness. If this becomes too difficult and you are getting swept away, you can place your attention back onto the breath and count up to twenty-one breaths.

Try to aim for twenty minutes, twice daily. If there is not enough time or you do not feel comfortable with this much, you can do five or ten minutes per day and work your way up from there. With time and practice, Shamata can become increasingly easier and more enjoyable.

When practicing Shamata, the great Buddhist Master **Tilopa** offers his **Six Words of Advice.** For many who may not know, Tilopa was a forefather of the Tibetan Buddhist sect, the Kagyu. He was a *Mahasiddha* meaning "one of great accomplishments" who many feel was a black-skinned sage from India. Below are his famous words of advice with my commentary.

Tilopa's Six Words of Advice

1) **"Don't recall... by letting go of what has passed."**
   If we do not let go of the past, this creates stagnation. Interestingly in alternative medicine, energy stagnation is the source of cancer. When energy is stagnant (qi), the blood becomes stagnant, resulting in disease. By responding to present events based on the past, it is like we are

the living dead, merely responding to phantasms that no longer exist. We become stuck and unable to move on, similar to a haunting ghost!

2) **"Don't imagine... by letting go of what may come."**
Sometimes in the present, something may look similar to the past. It is impossible for the exact same event to take place more than once. Based on preconditioned fears, worries, and expectations we react to any person or situation that appears similar to what caused the suffering (or happiness) previously.

3) **"Don't think... don't mentally capture and focus on a particular thought"**
By practicing letting go and maintaining peace of mind through Shamata and other spiritual practices, we slowly are able to have a full experience of the present moment.

4) **"Don't Examine... don't analyze every thought."**
We have a tendency to overanalyze an experience and miss the core meaning. It is difficult for us to perceive what is truly happening in any present moment when the mind is busy thinking and drawing conclusions.

5) **"Don't control... by trying to make events happen."**
Oftentimes, we overestimate how much control we have over our lives. Because we like to think we are in control of ourselves and our environment, we assume things will go how we planned. The

imagined result is often total happiness and no disappointment. However, time tends to show that things don't always go according to plan! In fact, if one looks closer, one will find themselves to be victims of the very thoughts and emotions they thought they had control over.

6) **"Rest the mind by making an effort to relax right now."**
You can rest the mind by making sincere efforts to do Shamata. Even when you are not doing sitting, this is a practice that can resonate and stay with you all day!

Cobra Breath

In ancient and modern cultures, the symbolism of the Cobra has played a large and intimate role in spiritual beliefs and traditions. The Cobra was unanimously used as iconic lore in ancient mythologies representing events taking place in the cosmos, activities of the deities and energetic occurrences in the body. In this context, more importantly, the Cobra is a symbol of the *Kundalini,*

meaning "coiled one." This is why the Cobra is seen as symbolic of spiritual awakening.

It is the female psycho-sexual energy or *Shakti* (the yin principle) that lies dormant at the base of the spine. Awakening the Kundalini from her slumber unites the female Shakti to her male counterpart, *Shiva* or the yang principle. Uniting both the yin and yang principles is the goal of the spiritual practitioner. To awaken the inner Cobra or Kundalini, means to awaken and expand your consciousness and obtain the clear light of wisdom. By practicing the Cobra Breath, we are following this essential philosophy. We are starting from the Yang principle (Shiva) going down as an adjunct to the traditional Yogic Kundalini practices.

Cobra Breath is an ancient practice stemming all the way back to the great Yogi, Mahavatar Agastar of the Tamil Dravidian Culture. This technology has been passed on generation after generation by many highly adept Yogis.

Its purpose is to purify the blood and rejuvenate the cells at a very high rate which also invigorates the body with fresh energies and serves to nullify karmic obscurations that obstruct the mind from witnessing its true nature. Cobra breathing also connects the conscious awareness with the subconscious resulting in enhanced dream recall capabilities.

When beginning this practice, it is best to start with twelve breaths per day for one hundred and twenty days. From here, you can transition to one hundred and forty-four repetitions per day for a total of one hundred and twenty days. It is important to note, that should you reach this point in practice, a suitable teacher is needed to further guide you in more advanced teachings.

Cobra breath should be approached with a full commitment to practice every day. Because of its unique transformative effects, the body cannot have interruptions. Missing a day or days at a time can work against your progress.

Below are the instructions for the beginning practice of Cobra Breath. I recommend that patience, consistency, and repetition are your intentions for this practice.

1) **Choose your posture**
   There are similarities with the seven positions of Shamata with only slight variations. Begin by sitting at the edge of a chair with your feet firmly planted or with your feet crossed. You can also sit at the edge of your bed if you prefer. While doing so, keep the back straight and the chin slightly tucked in and the **tongue placed at the roof of the mouth.**

2) **Make the Lion's Paw Mudra**
   Begin by placing the tips of the thumbs at the base joint of the ring fingers, and then fold the four fingers over the thumbs and rest both hands face down on your thighs or knees. This mudra helps relax the body and mind. It also reduces anger stored in the liver and overall stress caused by excessive worrying which affects the spleen/stomach.

3) Cobra Breathing

With eyes closed and eyebrows slightly raised, inhale, drawing the head upwards and looking up (internally) while internally chant the sound, *Om*. Next, hold the breath while looking up (internally) and internally chant the sound *Ah*. While continuing to hold the breath, look down (internally) and still intoning the sound *Ah* in the heart region of the body. While raising the head to a straight level, quickly sniff in additional air through the nose and place the tip of the tongue behind the bottom teeth.

4) Create hissing sound

With the tongue behind the lower teeth, slowly exhale and physically create the sound of a hissing *"Sssssssss"*, while also intoning mentally *HUM*.

5) Repeat steps 3 and 4

Steps 3 and 4 amount to one cycle. **As a reminder**, to receive the most benefits of cobra breathing, you should begin by practicing a minimum of twelve cycles per day for a total of one hundred and twenty days. From here, you can increase to one hundred and forty-four cycles per day for one hundred and twenty days.

Pumping the Abdomen to Aid Health (optional)

At the end of Step 3 and before beginning Step 4, you can continue to hold the breath and pump the abdomen in and out 7 times. At the same time, pull in the sphincter muscle. This additional step aids digestive fire and locks in the primal energy (sexual energy).

For Enhancing Dream Recall (Optional)

To further enhance spiritual revelations and/or dream recall after finishing the cobra breath lay on the right side in a fetal position for a minimum of 20 minutes. To come out of the fetal position/dream state one should do the Maahaah Yoga postures in the order of cobra pose, cat pose and lastly by sitting in the lion's pose. This is best done 4AM to 5AM.

Cobra Pose   Cat Pose   Lion Pose

Clear Light Meditation

Clear Light meditation is, in its own way, the hidden synthesis of the many methods of spiritual practices. Although technically, practicing the clear light meditation is a method itself, its aim is to gather the fruits that been harvested (qi or life-force) in the practitioner's spiritual path for the ultimate realization of one's true nature. When aiming to practice the clear light meditation, it is best done at the end of your practice routine to receive the most benefits. This is similar to launching a rocket. If there is not the necessary amount of fuel, a rocket will only be able to go so far. However, when there is enough fuel, a rocket is steady and can reach its intended destination. The "fuel" of your previous practices supply the qi or life-force needed to reach your ultimate destination, the clear light of wisdom. The practitioner is then able to open the door to the absolute realm landing one in a state of total Oneness.

Below are beginning instructions for practicing the Clear Light Meditation.

Part A

1) **Choose your posture**

Begin by sitting at the edge of a chair with your feet firmly planted or with your feet crossed. You can also sit at the edge of your bed if you prefer. Next, you can fold your hands and place them in your lap or place your palms on the knees. While doing so, keep the back straight and the chin slightly tucked in and the tongue placed at the roof of the mouth.

2) **Third Eye Gazing**

With your eyes closed, gently raise the eyebrows while looking slightly upwards at the area between the eyebrows or just above the eyebrows. From here, maintain your awareness on the lightest thing you can perceive. Remain in this position as long as you are comfortable, beginning with a few minutes at a time. With time and practice, you can sit an unlimited amount of time. Remember, more time spent doing spiritual practice isn't necessarily better. What is more important is that practice stays consistent. Even just five minutes a day performed consistently can make a greater difference than short-lived bursts of practice.

Part B

1) Intoning Mantra

After following steps 1 and 2 of Part A, inwardly intone either of these two mantras: *Om Mani Padme Hum* or *Om Ah Hum* (see glossary for mantra meanings). Mantra means "to save the mind." These mantras here are meant to erase negativity such as envy, hatred, laziness, lust, jealousy and/or any negativity that may be obstructing your happiness and wellbeing. There is no specific number of times you need to do these mantras.

(Questions were gathered from students after reading this section. For further explanation of terminology please refer to the Glossary)

Q: You say I can do Shamata all day. What do you mean by that?

A: In the Shamata practice, you can sit in the positions mentioned in the book, but once the mind is calm, you can maintain that state in any activity. One sits on a cushion to develop calmness of the mind and thoughts. Eventually, through continually practicing on the cushion, a person gets in touch with that state where the mind is calm, you can keep that same state through everyday life.

Q: Sometimes the emotions I feel are too much. How will I have the strength to bring this new path into my life?

A: Basically, by consistent practice and not being overly critical of oneself. On days that you feel that you don't have the strength, rather than trying to criticize yourself for not having the strength, just accept how you feel. However you feel, accept it and practice regardless of what your mental state is because emotions change like clouds. The mind is in a constant state of flux. When a person begins to think about something or become obsessive on a particular thought, stagnation takes place. It becomes mental stagnation when a person is constantly thinking about a painful or pleasurable event and not living in the present moment. This stagnation on a physical level usually becomes what we call cancer. So we can have a spiritual, mental and physical cancer. So, to answer the question again, if you feel your emotions are too much, just allow yourself to feel those emotions and don't try to stop those emotions. And that's Shamata actually. Just be whatever you are in that moment and it dissolves itself. If you're happy, be happy. If you're sad, be sad. Totally embrace that sadness. If you're angry, totally embrace that anger. You don't have to do anything but embrace the feeling and eventually it will go away. That is the essence of Shamata.

Q: What is the significance of the number one hundred and forty-four?

A: One hundred and forty-four is a symbolic number because one plus four and four equal nine. And that's coming from a male perspective, meaning the nine holes that need to be harmonized to reach a state of nirvana, or state of calmness. We lose energy through the two eyes, two ears, the mouth, the anus, the reproductive organs and through the two nostrils. From a female perspective twelve represents the twelve holes. Females have twelve holes which would include the nine holes plus the two breasts and the reproductive hole. Twelve x twelve = 144. The twelve in the female represents the twelve revolutions done in a particular Kriya Yoga practice. More explanation of this will be in volume two which will focus on the female principle of spirituality. We have these physical senses but when we become over-consumed or attached to any of those, that's what brings about suffering and illness on various different levels.

Q: When I do the practices, it is difficult to keep my posture for a long period of time without too much pain in my body. What can I do?

A: I recommend sitting in a chair, on the side of a bed or a couch. You can also sit cross-legged in bed and use a pillow against the backboard for extra support, keeping the back straight.

Q: You say Tilopa was a black-skinned sage. How come people don't know this?
A: It is not one hundred percent certain that Tilopa was black skinned. Many Indians are dark-skinned. African skin and dark Indian races have the same colored skin, but the subject is hardly brought up. Generally, there is a human tendency for dominant cultures to make spiritual images with their own racial color and usually, it is the more dominant culture in history that tends to rewrite images. For example, the British colonized and usurped Asiatic culture and obliterated, stole, hid and rewrote stories. Over time, people began to think everyone who did anything significant was white. There are different debates on the ancient race of the Dravidian culture. It is said that an Aryan race had taken over the culture and there was a cast system where the darker-skinned people, the original people of the land were considered lower in the cast system. We don't know for sure how long this system lasted and how much the original Dravidian culture was drowned out. But there are books that have been written that say even Gautama Buddha was black or aboriginal. Domineering cultures write the history books in a sense but it doesn't necessarily give the whole picture. But more importantly, all colors exist in everyone. Consciousness is without color, gender or sexual preference. Bluish green is the healing color for the liver that pacifies anger and is also the color of Divine Soul Culture. Blue is the water element and the color of the sky while green represents life and is seen all around in nature which has a natural calming effect. The Medicine Buddha, Kali, Durga, Shiva, Krishna and many others are blue or black.

SECTION 2

CAUSE OF SUFFERING: BUDDHISM AS A SOLUTION

Suffering

Twenty-Five hundred years ago Sakyamuni Buddha reached enlightenment. He expounded on the fact that human beings suffer because they are not in touch, nor do they understand their true nature (Buddha). This nature is covered up by obscurations (Kleshas) and the deluded mind. Attributes of this deluded mind are hatred, anger, greed or miserliness, ignorance, attachment, jealousy, and pride or egotism. These habitual tendencies are imprints in our own consciousness. What feeds these imprints is our Karma in the absolute sense. In the relative sense, we are being affected by messages from our mother's womb, society's messages, family, peer groups, the media such as television, radio, computers, and so forth that express various philosophical, political and religious doctrines of all types. We are constantly being programmed on what to believe and how to feel by someone else. Many views and

ideas that are constantly bombarding our consciousness are purposely done for economic and political benefit of a small group of individuals. Civilians of America, the most highly advanced, technological nation, have high rates of substance abuse, rape, divorce, mental health issues, physical health issues, obesity and murder. Most people in our population are taking psychotropic medication, smoking marijuana, using illegal substances or are abusing legal substances such as alcohol and cigarettes that lead to physical and legal destruction. Also, the stress of living the economic rat race that society has idealized for us, and trying to acquire new material items, to make one feel happy and accepted by peer groups and society, causes suffering. The fear of losing a job or having one's items stolen, health concerns, dealing with the death of loved ones and holding resentment against those that have done harm to us whether mentally, physically or spiritually is also suffering. Khenpo Karthar Rinpoche states that the Buddha called this the *suffering on top of suffering*. There is also the *suffering of change* and the *suffering of conditioned experience*. As long as we have a body (human or animal), there is suffering.

Lama Kathy Wesley from Columbus, Ohio states in her commentary on Sakyamuni's teaching, that "everything we experience whether it be happiness, sadness, pleasure or pain is perceived and framed in the mind." Interestingly, teachings in modern Allopathic (Western) medicine state that 70% of all illnesses have their origin in the mind. Asiatic medicine additionally states that the mind is in the heart and the heart is considered to be the emperor of the body and internal organs. This mind-body connection means that our mental condition can negatively or positively affect the energetic functioning of the whole person. Various illnesses can manifest and affect the organs based on a person's mental state. For example, anger is said to affect the liver and gall bladder, worry affects the spleen and stomach, fear affects the kidneys and bladder, grief affects the lungs and large intestines and excitement affects the heart and small intestine. If you feel a great deal of anger all of the time and have outbursts, this will tend to hurt the liver and gallbladder. If you experience a lot of grief, the lungs can fall into disrepair. This describes the mental disposition of most of our society today.

Listed below are the most common psychological tendencies of suffering humans experience and the organs that are energetically affected the most:

	Emotion	Organ
1)	Fear	Kidney, Heart
2)	Greed	Stomach, Spleen
3)	Laziness	Kidney, Heart
4)	Anger	Liver
5)	Envy	Kidney, Heart, Liver
6)	Worry	Spleen
7)	Sadness	Lungs
8)	Pride	Heart

The Four Noble Truths

Sakyamuni Buddha realized **Four Noble Truths** 2,500 years ago which are as follows:

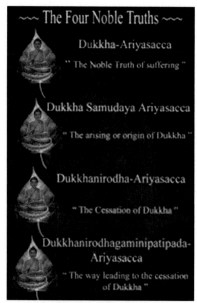

~~~ The Four Noble Truths ~~~

Dukkha-Ariyasacca

" The Noble Truth of suffering "

Dukkha Samudaya Ariyasacca

" The arising or origin of Dukkha "

Dukkhanirodha-Ariyasacca

" The Cessation of Dukkha "

Dukkhanirodhagaminipatipada-Ariyasacca

" The way leading to the cessation of Dukkha "

1) **The Truth of Suffering**. The Buddha states that all experiences and phenomena are ultimately unsatisfying.

2) **The truth of the Origin of Suffering.** The origin of suffering is essentially our impulses of clinging onto material and immaterial things and craving what is pleasurable. Not only is the origin of suffering from clinging and craving but it is also our aversion to what is not pleasurable. As long as we are not truly satisfied and continue to suffer, our cravings pull us back into *samsara,* or cyclic existence. We repeatedly experience the state of *becoming, rebirth, dissatisfaction*, and *death.*

3) **The truth of the cessation of suffering.** By putting an end to craving and clinging also means that we begin to have a clear view of becoming, rebirth, dissatisfaction, and death.

4) **The truth of the path that leads to liberation, (elimination of suffering).** The fourth noble truth is explained in a series of scientific, spiritual technology's that help bring about harmony (balance of body, spirit, and mind).This leads to clear, pure, awareness. And this is called the *Noble Eightfold Path.*

The Noble Eightfold Path

1) Right view
2) Right intention
3) Right speech
4) Right action
5) Right livelihood
6) Right effort
7) Right mindfulness
8) Right concentration

Taking refuge in **The Three Jewels**: *the Buddha, Dharma, and Sangha* is the first step on the Buddhist path which consists of taking refuge in all of Buddha's teachings.

The Three Jewels

1) **Buddha.** Taking refuge in the Buddha is an example of the sort of the life we should be living. When we take refuge, it is like taking cover under shelter. The Buddha truly represents our own Buddha nature. By walking this path, we consciously discover the inner Buddha within ourselves.

2) **Dharma**. Taking refuge in the Dharma means practicing and studying the Universal Truths that have been left for us by inheritance of the past and present Buddha's. (Dharma means universal truth.)

3) **Sangha**. Sangha translates as "assembly," or "community." When we take refuge in the sangha or our spiritual community, we can look to our peers and mentors for support along the way. With the proper guidance of the teachers and emotional support through our peers, we can feel safe that in case we fall down at times, there is someone there to help pick us back up. The community also helps us grow by always thinking of and considering other people's needs. The sangha makes it easier to work on our own vices and better ourselves in order to serve others even more.

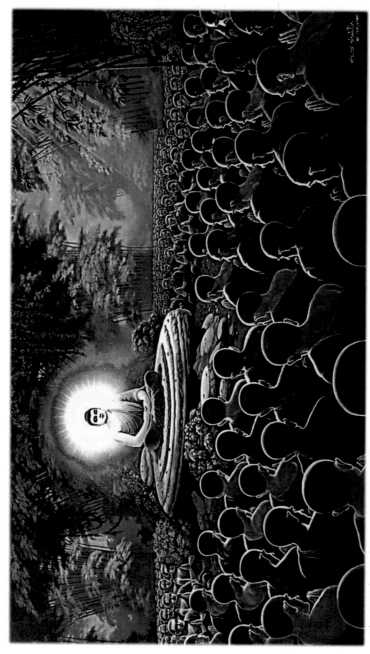

The Sangha is the community of like-minded individuals seeking truth and providing support to one another.

(Questions were gathered from students after reading this section. For further explanation of terminology please refer to the Glossary)

Q: If I'm not Buddhist, can I still do the practice?

A: Buddha means "supreme intelligence" or to be awake which is fitting for any human being. Anyone, Buddhist or not, can do the practice. These practices help bring someone to cultivate a "clear" mind, or to have clarity within one's self without obscurations such as greed, lust or ignorance. Scientific evidence shows that mindfulness creates a calming shift in the brain that can be of benefit to all people.

Q: You talk about clinging and craving and how it leads to more suffering and cyclic existence. But I do need money, food to eat and material things to survive. So what then?

A: You have to have right knowledge and right view. You need utilities, water, heat, clothes, and transportation. The reality is, you need these things so you should do what's necessary without breaking laws. You shouldn't do crimes. Much of crime is caused by commercialism that focuses on "self-image." Killing, stealing and criminal behavior feeds into the military industrial complex's vision for the masses. Particularly, minorities and low-income populations that are the fodder and the grass for the cows.

Q: What does it mean when the states of becoming, rebirth, dissatisfaction, and re-death go away. What is that like?

A: These categories don't exist anymore. Your mind is in a state of tranquility (Shamata) where there is no reaction and you're in a state of calm.

Q: When I follow the Eightfold Noble Path, it is difficult when other people around me think I'm stuck up or better than them. This causes a problem for me because I could lose friends and my reputation.
A: In regards to this matter, a Lama told me once, "A friend today, an enemy tomorrow." By following the Buddha, the Dharma, and the Sangha, you want to associate yourself with the Sangha or alike people for support. Spiritual teachers recommend not to move on the same path with others that don't follow the Dharma. Sangha (spiritual communities) are important to your mental and spiritual foundation so that you can become strong enough to not be affected by other people negative opinions and vibrations.

Q: Is it possible for a person to be like the Buddha if they suffer on a day-to-day basis?
A: Ending suffering has to do with awareness. When a person has more awareness they realize that everything is impermanent. By having right understanding, one is able to function on a day to day basis. From a Buddhist point of view, a person should experience the emotions that they have in the present moment. They should not get attached to the past or project into the future. If you project into the future, you're looking for a certain outcome or expectation which will cause anxiety which is a form of suffering.

SECTION 3

TRANSCENDING SUFFERING: MIND-BODY CONNECTION

TRANSCENDING SUFFERING: MIND-BODY CONNECTION

"All beings are confused and produce their future karma, falling into the ocean of life and death. They are trying to escape it, instead, they fall back into it. Why? Because the self-nature was not yet seen." -The Buddha

Spiritual Technology

There are many methods of spiritual technologies that one can do to harmonize negative and stagnant thoughts which hamper the Qi (life force) and manifest as disease on a physical level in the organs. As long as a person holds onto negative thoughts from the past, one cannot move on or live healthy in the present. The main point or focus in Buddhist practices is to remove obscurations and experience your true nature. We have previously examined the spiritual technologies that can be practiced in order to dissolve suffering such as Shamata, Cobra Breathing, and the Clear Light Meditation. Herein, we will be focusing more on transcending suffering through the use of more specific technologies that use the elemental qualities of sounds that have a direct impact on the connections between the body, mind, and spirit.

The eyes are classically considered to be windows of the soul. In Asiatic medical theory, they are the doorway to the liver and the liver is intimately connected to the heart. The emotion of anger is also a reflection of the liver's health. When someone experiences a lot of anger, this energy disrupts the heart and keeps the spiritual eye closed. This cycle leads people wanting to resorts to drugs and alcohol in order to have emotionally heightened experiences, but these are only temporary. Most times, people resort to drinking and doing drugs during the night when the body is meant to rest and sleep. In Asiatic medical theory, the liver is healthiest when it is allowed to sleep during the night. However, this is the time when many people want to stay up all night and party. This lifestyle can lead to an unhealthy liver, strong anger issues and leads to poor eyesight.

The correspondences in the first chart (Figure 1) contain the primordial healing sounds and mantras of the Buddhist and ancient Bon Traditions. Beginning with the *Bija* or syllables, you can see that there is a corresponding element, color, and two Buddhist Mantra sounds. Using either of the Bija or the Buddhist Mantras during meditation is entirely up to you. The five elements are the primordial qualities which all things are created from. These can further be perceived as the senses, our emotions, the mind and our overall character or persona. The balance of our elements greatly determines our overall health and character traits. By using the elements, we can see the underlying principles of the primordial sounds and wisdom.

The second chart (Figure 2) outlines what are called the Five Buddha Families and how these correspond to regions in the physical body and mental states. By understanding these correspondences, we can use this knowledge as a means of alleviating suffering. For example, the liver is said to be the organ that falls into disharmony when there is an excessive amount of anger. When anger is transformed by meditation, it is said to take the dual form of deities Asohbya (yang) and Locana (yin). Whether the primary root energy takes on a physical, emotional or deified form, these corresponding manifestations can be transformed by the use of spiritual technologies. To get started, recite the five Bijas which are: *Om, Yam, Ram, Bam, Lam. Or you can recite one of the following two* mantras: *Om Mani Padme Hum* and *Om Ah Hum So Ha.* Then repeatedly chant the sounds internally 11 times or 111 times with the eyes closed and the tongue at the roof of the mouth. By intoning these primordial sounds, you are working on healing the sufferings of the body, emotions and the mind.

Bija	Element	Color	Mantra 1	Mantra 2
Om	Spirit	White	Om	Om
Yam	Wind	Blue	Ma	Ah
Ram	Fire	Red	Ni	Hum
Bam	Water	Yellow	Padme	So
Lam	Earth	Green	Hum	Ha

Figure 1: Primordial Sounds and Wisdom

Buddha Family (Male/Female, Yin/Yang): Aspects of Mind	Physical States	Energetic Body (Mind)
Vajrochana/Dhatulsvari	Kidneys	Ignorance
Asohbya/Buddha Locana	Liver	Anger
Ratnasambhava/Mamaki	Heart	Pride
Amitabha/Padaravasini	Heart	Attachment
Amogasiddhi/Samayatara	Kidneys, Heart, Liver	Envy

Figure 2: Five Buddha Families

The Main Meridian Channels
of Chinese Medicine

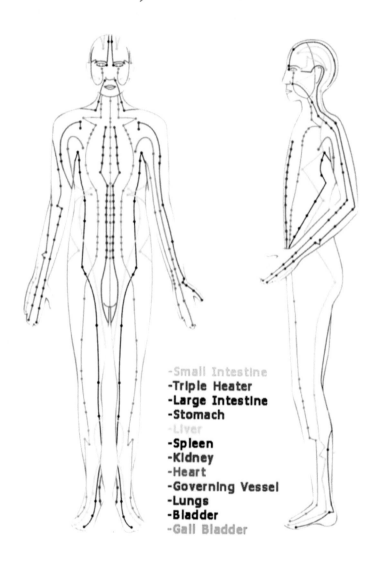

-Small Intestine
-Triple Heater
-Large Intestine
-Stomach
-Liver
-Spleen
-Kidney
-Heart
-Governing Vessel
-Lungs
-Bladder
-Gall Bladder

(Questions were gathered from students after reading this section. For further explanation of terminology please refer to the Glossary)

Q: I experience a lot of anger issues, so what do I do to remedy this with the use of healing mantras?

A: When one feels anger, in terms of medicine, anger affects the liver. In some schools, the liver and the heart are the same. The best Mantra to use is Om Mani Padme Hum. With constant repetition, the anger issue should dissolve. You have to keep applying this daily because anger is deeply rooted. It goes back to imprints that take place in the womb at the point of conception because the parents may have some levels of anger. That's when the anger is hereditary. Sometimes we may not be conscious of the anger and where it is coming from. So, we have to keep doing mantras and sitting. Various scenes may come up and release themselves. Sometimes we'll become angry and we don't know why. This is from our forefathers whom we inherited anger through our DNA. To help, whether you're consciously aware of the anger or not, you should do Om Mani Padme Hum daily in certain cycles. There are many different numbers of cycles but I usually prefer the cycles on the number eleven.

Q: How often should I use the mantras for healing?

A: Healing is a continual process. As I said before, we have issues that we're not consciously aware of in our present life or in the moment. Many times we suppress certain memories because the mind has a tendency to protect us when we experience stressful and painful situations. We compartmentalize the events, in other words, we suppress them. So, as we begin to do mantras, especially Om Mani Padme Hum or Om Ah Hum So Ha, we burn negative Karmas and all types of events we forgot about. The event could have been something that happened in kindergarten or middle school. The healing takes care of the Karmas of the mind stream in a backward sense. When this is taken care of, then the mantras help with events that are about to come in the future. There's a lot of talk about the ancestors, but there are upcoming generations to consider, so healing the present and the past heals the future. So, therefore, in my opinion, the prayers need to be done every day, as much as one is capable of doing it without causing harm to themselves, meaning that you're not doing so much mantra that you're not able to take care of your daily living. There are some side effects that can affect you physically such as feeling sluggish, the lack of excess of wanting to eat. When you're doing mantras, not only are you doing them for yourself, but you are also doing them for all sentient beings in our environment. When a person is suffering even a thousand miles away, we are suffering, too because we're all one mind stream. Everyone is connected even if we may not be consciously aware of it. As our consciousness becomes more awake, you can feel the pain and suffering of sentient beings everywhere.

Q: Can I help my loved ones with these mantras?

A: Of course. That's based on our intentions. Since everyone is all part of one mind stream, you can project your thought consciousness for a family member or any person. They get the benefit of your thoughts. The more you do it and the more focused on doing it, the more effective it is.

Q: What is a seed syllable?

A: A seed syllable, from my understanding, is a particular sound vibration that works on the energy vortexes or chakras. We place chakras at physical organs in the body. The origin of the seed syllables is in the mantra. So, certain tones and seed syllables are associated with a certain thought pattern. It's like music; you have scales, 12 in western, major and minor. The initial key is the seed syllable. When you hear C, it makes you feel a certain way. When you hear E, that makes you feel another way. When you hear B flat, it feels a different way. It brings about different moods and feelings. That's basically what a seed syllable is. From my understanding, it isn't much different than musical tones and vibrations associated with a certain feeling in a state of consciousness.

Q: What are the five Buddha Families?

A: The five families are states of consciousness that are subdivided and broken down so people can associate them. In Buddhist philosophy, they usually speak of Buddha families based on color, positive qualities, and negative qualities. In actuality, it's all one mind, but they break it down so a person can focus on a particular quality or aspiration such as fear, anger, worry, joy, lust, greed. And so, each one of those states of consciousness has a quality associated with it. Buddha means to be awake or enlightened and so if a person removes those five or six obscurations, then one is in the light of being awake.

SECTION 4

the world is a ghetto

The Aim of Meditation

In human society, there is a great amount of suffering caused by violence, racism, stereotyping, religious hatred, sexual abuse and the many crimes being committed such as homicide, rape, theft and financial scams. To make things worse, these committed acts created what Khenpo Karthar Rinpoche calls *suffering on top of suffering.* Many of the negative actions people make are merely responses to previous sufferings someone had undergone and this creates a cycle of unending pain. The misunderstanding many people have is in believing that by reacting to our sufferings negatively, this will somehow make things better and alleviate the pain we had previously felt before. Instead, negative actions only cause more suffering for ourselves and others. Violence breeds more violence, sexual abuse creates more sexual abusers, racism towards others creates more racism and the list goes on.

Much of the violence and suffering has an undeniable increase within ghetto communities. Many people are poor and do not have access to many worldly opportunities. But from a broader standpoint, the entire world could be seen as a ghetto. This is because of the very fact that everyone is suffering regardless of income, race, education or religious preference. When we realize this, we can understand that everyone is suffering from some kind of pain, even if the pain appears on the outside to be different. But, the wealthy have their own problems because no matter how much money they might have, they too will suffer from sickness, old age, and death. This kind of pain is a universal reality that we all will experience. In the world of cyclic existence, all of humanity suffers from loss, unhappiness, disease, aging, death.

In spiritual terms, Buddhism provides a philosophical reasoning that supports the concept of this world being a ghetto. This world is one of six. In Buddhism, there are six realms of the world that are a part of the Samsaric or cyclic existence. These are the *Realm of Human Beings* – the current "ghetto" you are consciously aware of and experiencing. The human realm is unique because it is a place of freedom and choice to decide how a person wishes to experience the world and create situations for future events or future *karmas* – these can be negative or positive. But it is not until we fully realize consciousness beyond the six realms that we are able to dissolve all future obscurations and transcend suffering completely.

In meditation, the aim is to increase our level of consciousness so we experience that which is beyond perceived suffering. In consciousness, there is no racism, violence, sexual abuse or any negativity. In our day to day living, attuning ourselves to higher vibratory levels brings peace and harmony in ourselves. The result has a positive impact on the lives of our loved ones. Statistically, in areas where people meditate more, there is less violence. Meditation also increases happiness, decreases clinging and craving for material wants, reduces stress and anxiety and improves your health. In time, you will realize there is no need to reach out for material gain because everything you need is inside you. Inner wealth and prosperity can be found through an increase in abundance of Qi (life force) and good health. Non-violence can be had through increasing peace in your state of mind. Racism and stereotyping can be obliterated by the view that all sentient beings are divine and have the potential to become a Buddha.

Our consciousness must transcend beyond color. Racism has had such a negative effect on the world consciousness which has resulted in so much suffering rooted in fear, envy, and greed.

"In Pure Consciousness...
        ...there is no color
            ....there is no gender
                ...there is no poverty
                    ...there is no suffering"

— K. A. Shakoor

My Mandala of World Peace

I pray for The Four Immeasurables for all humanity:

1) Appreciative Joy   2) Equanimity   3) Loving-kindness   4) Compassion

(Questions were gathered from students after reading this section. For further explanation of terminology please refer to the Glossary)

Q: What does Buddhism have to say about Heaven?

A: This is a very vast answer. And depending on what a person's state of understanding is, this is going to determine how a person views Heaven and Hell. In Buddhism, from my understanding, you really don't believe in anything unless you have a direct experience of it. For the sake of the answer, Heaven would be the state where a person has no suffering. Heaven and Hell is an internal mental state. I don't want to say there is a direct correlation of the Christian or Western concept of Heaven and Nirvana. But there's a state where a person is in total peace or a state of calmness. Islam or Salaam means "peace" and Dharsalaam means "city of peace." To be in a state of peace means that one has no desire and is content. Buddha said we suffer because we desire (meaning excessive craving). If a person has peace and is contented, then you don't have desires; and therefore, no suffering. So, that would be a state of heaven because in a Semitic sense, if a person goes to Heaven they are "favored" by God. That depends on the concept of a judge, prosecutor and a defense attorney which is based on Ancient Kemetic concepts. In Ancient Kemetic religions, the soul goes into the underworld and is judged, if your good deeds outweigh your bad deeds that determines whether you're going to the underworld or a peaceful place which we call heaven. That same type of drama plays itself over and over again based in different languages and cultures. In Zoroastrianism, they talk about it. Judaism talks about it. Christianity talks about it. Islam talks about it. Buddha talks about the heaven and hell *states.* These states actually exist inside ourselves. In Abrahamic religions, if you're blind in this life, you're blind in the next. This refers to being intellectually or spiritually blind. If a person is blind to the truth now, they're going to be blind to the truth later.

It has to do with being in a state of contentment. If I was to cross-reference between Semitic concepts versus Buddhist, Eastern or Indian Concepts, all of them are basically talking about being in a state of contentment. When one is content, one has no desire. When one is content in the life that they are in, there's no envy and you're not worried about what somebody else has. If you're content with yourself you don't have low self-esteem so certain kinds of fears don't come up. This eliminates certain kinds of unhealthy fear as well as worry and anger. Basically, everyone is looking for peace and peace of mind. Everyone is trying different routes. Some people think that if they have all the money and materialism, they'll have peace so they pursue that. Some people think that if they have a good love life, they'll have peace and all the derivatives of that: a good love life, good physical health, knowing everything there is to know and great spiritual power. This can go on and on, but if a person is contented in the state that they are in and accept themselves, that becomes the beginning of peace. Even with negative qualities, the key is that you have to accept them and then not punish yourself. So, from a Western concept, it's not a matter of whether God forgives you, it's a matter of whether you can forgive yourself. Now we are correlating with what Buddhism teaches that everything is dealing with the self. You see people every day in our court systems and in AA meetings that can't forgive themselves even though the ministers and preachers and everyone say that you're forgiven. "You've been saved," and all the other types of clichés and yet people still have torment. People are on psychotropic medicines like never before. Suicide rates are like never before. Murder rates are like never before. Alcoholism and drug use are like never before because people have not forgiven themselves. You can't forgive others until you truly forgive yourself. From a therapeutic point of view, most people are seeing a therapist or some kind of healing with the mind usually because they can't forgive themselves or are not able to forgive another person or persons from doing some type of harm to them at some point.

Note: I will go into further detail about Heaven and Hell and after death states (Bardo) in Ghetto Sutras, Volume III.

Q: Experiencing conscious awareness sounds like a wonderful thing, but in the real world, I don't see how I can stay aware all the time. What do you say to that?
A: My answer to that is not to worry about it. Just do what you can, and make a sincere effort every day to do Shamata, which is the basis of calming the mind. As the mind becomes calmer, it becomes more aware. Shamata not only allows us to calm the mind, but it keeps us in the moment. The more we do Shamata, whether you're sitting on the couch or whatever, eventually you do it more and more until you get to a point where you're in the present moment all the time. That is being in a state of peace. If a person has a mental disruption it is difficult to be in the present moment. That's why I say don't worry about it. Just do what you can do and make the effort. In time you

will begin to experience those states, and you'll experience them without even thinking about it. If you sit around wondering when it's going to happen, then it won't happen. Don't think about getting to some final point because there is no final point. Everything is in a continual flow. To my mind, that's what enlightenment is. There is no getting to some point and then that's it because that becomes stagnation. Everything is in constant motion, because when things stop, that's death. So, I say don't worry about it because at some point you're going to get there.

Q: if I want more peace in my life... How can I successfully respond to violent acts towards me without using violence?

A: Again, from the perspective of sitting, as one's mind becomes calm one becomes able to see what it is that you are doing that's putting you into a violent situation. By having a clearer consciousness and a clearer mind you'll be able to see that, and you'll change the rhythm. So, repeated acts begin to change themselves, but there again, it comes from a change in the mind. But the mind can't change if it's not clear, it has to be clear to know what to do. In Shamata, calming the mind is the first step. Once the mind is calm then clear insight begins to come. You then have the insight and clarity, and just by that awareness, it starts to change the vibration. But definitely, once you have the view, and you're able to hold the view, then you're ready to take action. And that's the Dzogchen kind of view. Holding the view and then taking action. So, first, you calm the mind, and through calming the mind clear insight comes. Then the action will take place based on the clarity of the mind. So now, if I use a Funkadelic concept that I want you to use, they said: "free your mind and your ass will follow." So, if you can get clear insight then automatically your action is going to be a result of your mind. We act based on what our mind dictates. Even if we are unconscious, it is still consciousness, we are just not aware of it. We are still acting off it, even if you're not conscious of it!

Q: Can you describe the realm of the Hungry Ghosts?
A: I'll say this about Hungry Ghosts. Hungry ghost is a deficiency, it's from when a person lacks nurturing. I'm going to speak about Hungry Ghosts from the perspective of consciousness, not from a realm outside the human mind. I'm not saying there's not a realm of Hungry Ghosts, but right now I'm talking about the mental perspective of Hungry Ghosts from my understanding. It comes from a person who did not have nurturing, and usually, the person was either mentally or physically abandoned by the mother. We can put the father in there too, but the mother is primary. So, as a result, no matter what they do in life, nothing satisfies them because they didn't get that basic nourishing as a child. So, no amount of money or relationships satisfies them. This can manifest as a sexaholic, a shopaholic, gambling addictions, and drug and alcohol addiction. We're using a relative term for a psychological description; it's like having a hole in the heart. It's like having a bucket of water and throwing it into the Grand Canyon. You'll never fill the Grand Canyon up, even if it's a bathtub of water. So, no matter what that person gets it is never enough because they didn't get that initial imprint of nurturing. The personality is shaped by either age five or seven, depending on what school of thought you're dealing with.

Q: If there is no racism, violence, or negativity in pure consciousness, as you say, then what does it feel like to be in that state?

A: You will be in a state where you become more sensitive and feel the pain and suffering off everything around you. Most people never get to self-liberation because they are in a state of reaction rather than responding from a clear state.

CONCLUSION

The purpose of Ghetto Sutras Volume I is to introduce the concept that obscurations (greed, envy, hate, fear, gluttony) are the cause of human suffering. We're not aware of the fact that we attach to impermanent things. We attach value to an impermanent reality as a form of permanence. We have been seduced by the corporate world we live in (a military industrial complex), where everything is based on buying and selling commodities, and even humans. The human self-image is manufactured by the artificial images created by the media which in turn is an extension of the same corporate and military industrial complex. Constantly exposing children to these images imprint ideas and thought concepts that lead to self-destructive lifestyles. Fulfilling this image sold by the media is largely unattainable based on the nation's economic and social structure. Hence, we can see a constant increase of children, adolescents and adults cheating, raping, stealing, and murdering in their own communities attempting to attain this false illusory image which in turn creates dysfunctions in the mind, body, and spirit (mental and physical health). Because of this, our whole society is severely affected. This is the ghetto!

Intrinsically we are all one. We are a collective mind-stream who want peace, justice, love, respect, comfort, success, wealth, and freedom. However, in this ghetto the challenge becomes: how to live in harmony with ourselves and others, especially, those who look different than us?

By practicing the simple techniques of mindfulness and meditation we can balance the obscurations and attain clear vision which becomes the foundation of any successful action that we take in life. This is the core message of this book and Universal Buddhism. By following the universal concepts of Buddhism we can lead a more meaningful, balanced and fulfilling life.

The Ghetto Sutras, Volume II:
"When The Mother Suffers All Humanity Suffers"

The focus of this volume will be the feminine and matriarchal aspect of religion and its importance to this ghetto.

GLOSSARY

Agastyar: one of the greatest energetic teachers of the ancient Indian (Tamil) civilization. Agastyar contributed books in the area of physical sciences chemistry and biology, herbalism, medicine and spiritual sciences, particularly yogic.

Asohbya or Aksobhya (Vajrasattva): An aspect of the mind that deals with being free from aversion and anger. One of the Five Buddha Families. Color representing the energetic and mind-body: blue. Element representing the physical body and the organs that are related: Water.

Amitabha: one of the aspects of the mind that deals with being free from attachment. One of the Five Buddha Families. Color representing the energetic and mind-body: red. Element representing the physical body and the organs that are related: Fire.

Amogasiddhi: one of the Five Buddha Families that represent freedom from envy. Color representing the energetic and mind-body: green. Element representing the physical body and the organs that are related: Air/Wind.

Brahma: the creative aspect of God according to Vedic Religion. Some Vedic schools worship him as the one and only God.

Bon: the indigenous religion of the Tibetan region. Bon is very shamanistic in its practices. Bon practitioners follow the Buddha of 18,000 years ago, the Buddha Shenrab.

Some scholars say Bon is of Zoroastrian, Vedic or Kashmiri Buddhist origin. The 14th Dalai Lama has recognized Bon as the fifth school of Tibetan Buddhism.

Buddha: in translations, it has many meanings: To be awakened, supreme intelligence, enlightened and realized. These are some of the most common meanings. These meanings can be attributed to any human being. Classical Buddhism states all beings have the Buddha nature in them. This means that our consciousness is already clear or enlightened by nature. But it is the Obscurations (the agitated mind states, the deluded mind, and habitual tendencies) that prevent us from being in a constant enlightened state. These obscurations lead to suffering which can be done away by taking Refuge.

Calm Abiding (Shamatha): is another name for mindfulness. This is the basis and foundational meditative technique that leads to clear insight. See Shamatha.

Buddhism: in Sanskrit Buddhi means intelligent or Dharma-existence. In Tibetan, Buddhism means custom (Chos,) or custom of the divine beings (lha). A Chospa is one who follows Indian Buddhism. And Bonpo is one who follows the Buddhist teaching of the Buddha Tonpa Shenrab of 18,000 years ago. A lesser known story of Buddhism is that its doctrines originated in the Tamil Dravidian civilization from various Mahasiddhas. According to the Gaudiya Vaishnava sect in India, Shakyamuni Buddha is seen as the 9th incarnation of Vishnu, the compassionate quality of the Universal Source. It is interesting to note that Sakyamuni Buddha was enlightened in Bodgaya, India. Many enlightened sages that shaped modern Buddhism were from India:

Nagarjuna, Tilopa, Naropa, Atisa and Sakyamuni Buddha who was born on the border of India and Nepal.

Another view of Buddhism's origin is presented by the scholar Cheik Anta Diop his research shows that Asian Buddhism came from the Amen-Ra priests in Ancient Egypt (Kemet) who introduced this through trade and travel into India, Iran, and Afghanistan. My view is that the continents of East Africa, Australia, Indonesia, Malaysia, East India, and South Eastern Asia were all connected and there was a universal philosophy and culture that existed. It could be said that those people were "Oceanic" (meaning of many color combinations and hues that we don't commonly see today.) As the collective mind descended into more material attachment the high sciences that they developed were used for destructive means that eventually caused major continental shifts, climatic changes, and divisions among people (caste systems, sexism, racism, nationalism, etc.)

The Buddhism that is most commonly known is the Buddhism under Sakyamuni Buddha, who was born in Lumbini near India and Nepal around 563 B.C.E. He was born as a prince. He renounced his kingdom at age twenty-nine and went on a search for enlightenment. At age 35 he had a divine realization that the cause of suffering and pain was due to human desire. To alleviate this problem he purported a doctrine based on the Four Noble Truths: 1) The truth of suffering, the 2) truth of the origin of suffering, the 3) Truth of the cessation of suffering, and the 4) Truth of the path to the cessation of suffering. By taking refuge in the Buddha (see Buddha,) the Dharma (see Buddha and Dharma,) and Sangha (see Buddha Dharma and Sangha,) one will reach liberation from the endless rounds of mental delusion. Meditation can be divided into two parts: Shamata and Clear Insight. Through the practice of 1) Shamata one's mind becomes calm. This leads to 2) Clear Insight, which is your personal mental clarity of thoughts and actions taking on the qualities of the eightfold path: 1) Correct or Right Views, 2) Correct Or Right intentions, 3) Correct or Right speech, 4) Correct or Right behavior, 5) Correct or Right living, 6) Correct or Right effort, 7) Correct or Right attitude, and 8) Correct or Right concentration.

The system of Buddhism is divided into three major paths, ways, or yanas: 1) Hinayana, this is where an individual focuses on their own enlightenment, 2) Mahayana, which means delaying your own enlightenment to help other beings reach liberation (Maha means greater path.) and 3) Vajrayana (thunderbolt way) this is combining both of the previous yanas in a very unique way to help sentient beings. Saykamuni Buddha taught that there are 84,000 different minds so no one method or presentation is going to work for everyone.

Chi (Qi): the life force that is the prime mover in the external universe and the prime mover of blood in the human body.

Christianity: The religion based on the life and teachings of Jesus Christ. Christians believe that Jesus Christ is the Messiah, sent by God. They believe that Jesus, by dying and rising from the dead justified the sin of Adam and thus redeemed the world allowing all who believe in him to enter heaven. Christians rely on the Bible as the inspired word of God.

Dharma: the absolute universal truth. (See Buddhism)

Dravidian: an Afro-Asiatic people that are considered by many to be the original inhabitants of India. These were the founders of yogic sciences that followed the matriarchal religious systems. Tamil is one of the major languages of these people.

Dzogchen: "Great Perfection", also called Atiyoga, is a tradition of teachings in Tibetan Buddhism aimed at attaining and maintaining the natural primordial state or natural condition. It is a central teaching of the Nyingma school of Tibetan Buddhism and of Bon.

Durga: is the principal form of the Mother Goddess in Vedic religions. She is known by a variety of names: including Amba, Ambika, Jagadamba, Parvathi, Shakti, Adishakti, Adi Parashakti and Devi. Durga is regarded by Vedic as the root cause of creation, sustenance, and annihilation. She is pure energy (referred to as "Shakti" in Sanskrit and Vedic religious context). Being innately formless (known as Adi Parashakti), she manifests herself within the gods and demi gods so that she may fulfill the tasks of the universe via them. At times of distress, she manifests herself in divine form to protect the world.

Five Buddha Families: They symbolize five different human aspects of the neurotic mind (obscurations) that we must strive to transform into light consciousness: 1) Vairochana (ignorance/wisdom,) 2) Asohbya (anger/humility,) 3) Ratnasambhava (pride/giving,) 4) Amitabha (attachment/compassion,) 5) Amogasiddhi (jealousy/fearlessness [total trust and faith in oneself, one's guru, the divine or the void].) [Refer to the Secret Doctrines of the Tibetan Book of the Dead for more detail]

*Funk: denoting a type of dance music that combines funk with elements such as highly amplified guitars and heavy drum beats derived from rock.

*Funkadelic: is an American band that was most prominent during the 1970s. The band and its sister act Parliament, both led by George Clinton, pioneered the funk music culture of that decade. (Recommended albums: *Free Your Mind... and Your Ass Will Follow*, 1970; *Maggot Brain*, 1971; *One Nation Under a Groove*, 1978)

*George Clinton: George Clinton is an American singer, songwriter, bandleader, and music producer. He was the principal architect of P-Funk, the mastermind of the bands Parliament and Funkadelic during the 1970s and early 1980s, and launched a solo career in 1981. He has been cited as one of the foremost innovators of funk music, along with James Brown and Sly Stone. He was inducted into the Rock and Roll Hall of Fame in 1997, alongside 15 other members of Parliament-Funkadelic.

*Note: The author includes these three definitions because he was heavily influenced by George Clinton's Buddhist ideas in his music. Funk music is mantra driven due to its heavy use of repetition.

Guru: is a Sanskrit term that connotes someone who is a "teacher, guide, expert or master" of certain knowledge or field. The term also refers to someone who primarily is one's spiritual guide, who helps one to discover the same potentialities that the *guru* has already realized. A true guru exists in each human being once obscurations are removed. The true teacher is within us.

Matthew 6:22 "The eye is the lamp of the body. If your vision is clear, your whole body will be full of light."

Quran 50:22 Shakoor: "so far you have been in a state of ignorance and mindfulness. Now we have removed from thee thy veil, and there will be nothing but pure light."

<u>Hatha Yoga</u>: Hatha yoga is the most widely practiced form of yoga in America. It is the branch of yoga which concentrates on physical health and mental well-being. Hatha yoga uses bodily postures (*asanas*), breathing techniques (*pranayama*), and meditation (*dyana*) with the goal of bringing about a sound, healthy body, and a clear, peaceful mind. There are nearly 200 hatha yoga postures, with hundreds of variations, which work to make the spine supple and to promote circulation in all the organs, glands, and tissues. Hatha yoga postures also stretch and align the body, promoting balance and flexibility.

<u>Hungry ghosts</u>: one of the six states of human consciousness that imitates greed, people that are never in a state of mental peace. There is an emptiness in their energetic heart. An example of this is overeating, gambling, shopping, and drug addictions. Energetic vampires, people who thrive off other people's energy.

<u>Islam</u>: Means "a state of peace" in the Arabic language coming from the word "salaam" meaning peace (like Jerusalem, meaning city of peace, and a Muslim, meaning "one of great peace.") The religious faith of Muslims,

based on the words and religious system founded by the prophet Muhammad and taught by the Quran, the basic principle of which is absolute submission to a unique and personal God, Allah (which means "the absolute unknowable beyond human comprehension." In Aramaic, the language of Jesus, God is called "Allah")

Jainism: a dualistic religion founded in the 6th century B.C. as a revolt against current Vedic doctrines and emphasizing the perfectibility of human nature and liberation of the soul especially through asceticism and nonviolence toward all living creatures. Mahatma Gandhi was a Jain. Martin Luther King was greatly influenced by the non-violent teachings of Gandhi.

Judaism: The religion of the Israelites of the Bible and of the Jews of today, based on the teachings of the Torah. Judaism involves the belief in one God, whose chosen people are the Jews. Abraham is considered the founder of Judaism, although Moses, who delivered the laws of God to the Israelites, is also an important figure.

Kali: A Vedic goddess who is the mighty aspect of the goddess Durga. The name Kali is derived from the Sanskrit "Kālá", or time. She, therefore, represents Time, Change, Power, Creation, Preservation, and Destruction. "Kali" also means "the black one", the feminine noun of the Sanskrit adjective Kālá. Her earliest appearance is that of a destroyer, principally of evil forces. Various Shakta Vedic cosmologies, as well as Shākta Tantric beliefs, worship her as the ultimate reality, or Brahma. Devotees worship Kāli as a benevolent mother goddess. She is often portrayed standing or dancing on her consort, the Vedic god Shiva, who lies calm and prostrate beneath her. Kali is worshiped by Vedics throughout India but particularly South India, Bengal, and Assam.

Karma: this word has many definitions, but without going into all of its meanings it is basically a person's present reality based on their past thoughts, intentions, and actions. Also, a person's future reality will be based on their present thoughts, intentions, and actions. A person's rebirth will also be determined likewise.

Karmapa: Karmapa means "the one who carries out buddha-activity" or "the embodiment of all the activities of the buddhas". In the Tibetan tradition, great enlightened teachers are said to be able to consciously control their rebirth in order to continue their activity for the benefit of all sentient beings. Ogyen Trinley Dorje (born June 26, 1985) is the 17th Karmapa. The Karmapa is head of the Karma Kagyu school, one of the four main schools of Tibetan Buddhism.

Khenpo Karthar Rinpoche: is a senior lama of the Karma Kagyu school of Tibetan Buddhism. As of 2016 he serves as abbot of Karma Triyana Dharmachakra (KTD) Monastery in Woodstock, NY.

Krishna: A god, worshiped across many traditions of religion in a variety of different perspectives. Krishna is recognized as the complete and or as the Supreme God in his own right by some Vedic schools. However, some others worship Krishna as one of the most widely revered and popular of all Vedic deities.

Kundalini: In yogic theory, is a primal energy, or *shakti*, located at the base of the spine. Different spiritual traditions teach methods of "awakening" kundalini for the purpose of reaching spiritual enlightenment. Kundalini is described by some as lying "coiled" at the base of the spine, represented as either a goddess or sleeping serpent waiting to be awakened. In modern commentaries, Kundalini has been called an unconscious, instinctive or libidinal force or "mother energy or intelligence of complete maturation". However, my research shows that Kundalini means "to uncover" veils of consciousness, similar to Buddha Nature, the pure unadulterated consciousness of a human being.

Lama David Bole: he is a fully ordained monk (Gelong) and completed the traditional three years and three-month retreat in the Karma Kagyu lineage of Tibetan Buddhism. He studied meditation under the direction of the renowned retreat master Khenpo Karthar Rinpoche. Lama David currently serves as the resident teacher for the Gainesville Karma Thegsum Choling (KTC), a branch of the Karma Triyana Dharmachakra Monastery (KTD) in Woodstock, N.Y., the North American seat of H.H. the 17th Gyalwa Karmapa.

Lama Kathy Wesley: serves at the Columbus Karma Thegsum Chöling Meditation Center as its practice coordinator, and travels to other Buddhist centers throughout the country to teach. She has been a student of Khenpo Karthar Rinpoche since 1977. She participated in the first three-year retreat led by Khenpo Rinpoche at Karme Ling Retreat Center in upstate New York, and thus earned the title of "retreat lama."

Mahasiddha: "great adept" is a term for someone who embodies and cultivates the "siddhi of perfection". They are a certain type of yogin/yogini recognized in Vajrayana Buddhism. Mahasiddhas were tantra practitioners or tantrikas who had sufficient empowerments and teachings to act as a guru or tantric master. A Siddha is an individual who, through the practice of sādhanā, attains the realization of siddhis, psychic and spiritual abilities and powers. Their historical influence throughout the Indian subcontinent and the Himalayas was vast and they reached mythic proportions as codified in their songs of realization and hagiographies, or namtars, many of which have been preserved in the Tibetan Buddhist canon.

Mantra: is a sacred utterance, a numinous sound, a syllable, word or phonemes, or group of words in Sanskrit believed by practitioners to have psychological and spiritual powers. A mantra may or may not have a syntactic structure or literal meaning.

Medicine Buddha: Medicine Buddha is a Buddha Doctor on the energetic level. He is an enlightened being who has unbiased compassion for all living beings. He protects living beings from physical and mental sickness and other dangers and obstacles and helps them to eradicate the three poisons: attachment, hatred, and ignorance, which are the source of all sickness and danger.

Mudras: A series of hands, wrist, and finger manipulations used in various rituals and prayers. Most commonly associated with Buddhist and Vedic practices. Mudras can block, constrict, open, or direct subtle energy, internally or externally. Subtle energy can be also known as Qi, Rlung, Prana, or Nafas.

Ngondro: The Tibetan term Ngöndro (known in Sanskrit as pūrvaka) refers to the preliminary, preparatory or foundational practices or disciplines common to all four schools of Tibetan Buddhism and also to Bon. They precede the Generation stage and Completion stage.

The term *ngöndro* literally denotes meanings in the range of "something that goes before, something which precedes." The preliminary practices establish the foundation for the more advanced and rarefied Vajrayana sādhanā which are held to engender realization. Of the four foundations of Vajrayana Buddhism: refuge, prostrations, mantras, and guru yoga, Ngondro is commonly known as prostrations.

The practice of Ngöndro is a complete and sufficient practice of the spiritual path, and that it can take the practitioner all the way to full enlightenment.

Ratnasambhava: one of the aspects of the mind that deals with pride. One of the Five Buddha Families. Color representing the energetic and mind-body: gold/yellow. Element representing the physical body and the organs that are related: Earth.

Refuge: The method by which we can transcend suffering. The Sakyamuni Buddha, the enlightened Buddha of this yuga or time period, stated that by taking Refuge one can be freed from suffering. Taking Refuge is accomplished in three parts: 1) by taking Refuge in The Buddha (which can mean either to ultimately trust in yourself and examine your own mind in detail, or to follow the examples of the historical Buddha of 2,500 years ago, or to follow the instructions of a living enlighten teacher like the 17th Karmapa or the 14Th Dalai Lama.) 2) by taking Refuge in the Dharma, meaning the written sayings (sutras) of the Sakyamuni Buddha or texts of any great teacher (lama,) saint, or realized personality of any Buddhist tradition. 3) by taking Refuge in the Sangha, which means association with like-minded persons. This method of taking Refuge helps a person transform negative agitated mind states (anger, hate, envy, greed, laziness, fear, worry, resentment, etc.) into compassion, patience, courage, enthusiasm and forgiveness.

Samadhi: A state where the mind is in an unwavering total place of calm.

Samsara: the vicious cycle of mental confusion and conflicting emotions. In Buddhism there are six basic types of mental conflicts 1) Pride, 2) Envy, 3) Passion, 4) Ignorance, 5) Greed, 6) Hatred.

Shakti: In Vedic, Shakti means "power" or "empowerment," is the primordial cosmic energy and represents the dynamic forces that are thought to move through the entire universe. Shakti is the concept, or personification, of divine feminine creative power, sometimes referred to as 'The Great Divine Mother' in Vedic.

Shiva: Sanskrit meaning "The Auspicious One" is one of the three major deities of Vedic. He is the chief deity within Shaivism, one of the three most influential denominations in contemporary Vedic. He is one of the five primary forms of God in the Smarta tradition and "the Transformer"

At the highest level, Shiva is regarded as limitless, transcendent, unchanging and formless. Shiva also has many benevolent and fearsome forms. In benevolent aspects, he is depicted as an omniscient yogi who lives an ascetic life on Mount Kailash, as well as a householder with wife Parvati and his two children, Ganesha and Kartikeya, and in fierce aspects, he is often depicted slaying demons. Shiva is also regarded as the patron god of yoga and arts.

Tai Chi Chuan: is an internal Chinese mind-body practice for both its health benefits and its defense training. It is also typically practiced for a variety of other personal reasons: achieving greater longevity, demonstration competitions, and competitive wrestling in the format of pushing hands (tui shou). As a result, a multitude of training forms exist, both traditional and modern, which correspond to those aims with differing emphasis. Some training forms of t'ai chi ch'uan are especially known for being practiced with relatively slow movements. The Maahaah-Rooh form I developed is derived from the Dong (Tong) Yang family style.

Vairocana: one of the aspects of the mind that deals with ignorance. One of the Five Buddha Families. Color representing the energetic and mind-body: white. Element representing the physical body and the organs that are related: Space.

Vedic: The oldest and most authoritative body of sacred rituals, the culture of ancient India. Vedic texts were composed in Sanskrit and gathered into four collections. People still practice the Vedic religion and culture today worldwide.

Vishnu: Preservation and compassionate aspect of God in the Vedic religion. Many humans have been emanations of Vishnu in the flesh such as Krishna and Buddha.

War: (originally called Eric Burdon and War) is an American funk band from Long Beach, California, known for the hit songs "Spill the Wine", "The World Is a Ghetto", "The Cisco Kid", "Why Can't We Be Friends?", "Low Rider", and "Summer". Formed in 1969, War was a musical crossover band which fused elements of rock, funk, jazz, Latin, rhythm and blues, and reggae. Their album *The World Is a Ghetto* was the best-selling album of 1973. The band also transcended racial and cultural barriers with a multi-ethnic line-up.

Wind: Subtle energy that moves in the body through energetic channels commonly known as meridians. Wind can affect the physical organs and the mind. This energy can also be known as Qi, Rlung, Prana, or Nafas.

Zoroastrianism: or more natively Mazdayasna, is one of the world's oldest religions, "combining a cosmogonic dualism and eschatological monotheism in a manner unique among the major religions of the world." Ascribed to the teachings of the Iranian Prophet Zoroaster (or Zarathustra), he exalted their deity of wisdom, Ahura Mazda, (*Wise Lord*) as its Supreme Being. Leading characteristics, such as messianism, heaven and hell, and free-will influenced other religious systems, including Second Temple Judaism, Gnosticism, Christianity, and Islam.

RECOMMENDED READING

A People's History of the United States, Howard Zinn, 2005, Harper Perennial Modern Classics

African Religions & Philosophy, John S. Mbiti, London: Heinemann Educational Publishers, 1990

A Return to Love: Reflections on the Principles of "A Course in Miracles", Marianne Williamson, London: Harper Collins Publishers, 1996

Awakening Into Oneness, Arjuna Ardagh, Sounds True Inc., 2007

Babaji and the 18 Siddha Kriya Yoga Traditions, Marshall Govindan, Montreal: Kriya Yoga Publications, 1991

Before the Mayflower: A History of Black America, Lerone Bennett, Chicago: Johnson Publishing Company Inc., 1969

Bhagavad Gita: As it is, Swami A.C. Bhaktivedanta Prabhupada, New York: Macmillan Publishing, 1972

Black Indians: A Hidden Heritage, New York: Atheneum Books for Young Readers, William Loren Katz, 2012

Black Man of the Nile, Yosef ben-Jochannan, Black Classic Press, 1996

The Destruction of Black Civilization: Great Issues of a Race from 4500 B.C. to 2000 A.D., Chancellor Williams, Chicago: Third World Press, 1994

Dragon Rises, Red Bird Flies: Psychology & Chinese Medicine, Leon I. Hammer, United States: Eastland Press, 2005

Health Through Balance: An Introduction to Tibetan Medicine, Yeshi Dhonden, Ithaca, N.Y., USA: Snow Lion, 1986

How to Love, Thich Nhat Hanh, Parallax Press, 2014

Introduction to Tibetan Buddhism, David N. Bole, Ph.D. – 4 DVD set available at the http://davidbole.com/store

Karma Chakmes Mountain Dharma, Volumes I-IV, Khenpo Karthar Rinpoche, KTD Publications, 2005

Maahaah-Yoga, Health, Healing and Happiness, 2007, Jannah Press, K.A. Shakoor – free set available at http://www.maahaah-rooh.com/#!1/cn1

Nine Ways of Bon: Excerpts from Gzi-Brjid, David L. Snellgrove, Great Eastern Book Co, 1967, Issued As V. 18 of London Oriental Series

Relationships That Work: The Power Of Conscious Living, David Wolf, Ph.D., San Rafael, CA, USA: Mandala Publishing, 2008

Secret Doctrines of the Tibetan Books of the Dead, Detlef Ingo Lauf, Shambhala Publications, 1977

Shingon: Japanese Esoteric Buddhism, Taiko Yamasaki, Shambhala, 1988

Siddhartha, Hermann Hesse, Bantam, 1981

Spiritual Warrior (Series), Volumes I-IV, Swami Krishnapada, Hari-Nama Press, 1998

Spiritual Liberation: Fulfilling Your Soul's Potential, Michael Bernard Beckwith, Atria Books/Beyond Words, 2009

Stress Management and Relaxation Training: Guided Meditation and Body, David N. Bole, Ph.D. - CD set available at http://davidbole.com/store

The African Origin of Civilization: Myth or Reality, Cheikh Anta Diop, Chicago Review Press, 1989

The Cult of Tara, Stephan Beyer, University of California Press, 1978

The Essential Rumi, Jalal al-Din Rumi, Castle Books, 1997

The Human Situation, Harvey Jackins, Rational Island Publishers, 1973

The Jerusalem Bible, Alexander Jones, Image, 2000

The Power of Now, Eckhart Tolle, Namaste Publishing, 2004

The Serpent Power - The Secrets of Tantric and Shakti Yoga, Arthur Avalon, Dover Publications, 1974

The Tibetan Book of Great Liberation, W.Y. Evans-Wentz, Oxford, 1972

The Tibetan Book of Living and Dying, Sogyal Rinpoche, San Francisco, CA, USA: Harper San Francisco, 2012

The Tibetan Book of the Dead, Graham Coleman and Thupten Jinpa, London: Penguin Classics, 2010

The Untethered Soul: The Journey Beyond Yourself, Michael A. Singer, Oakland, CA, USA: New Harbinger Publications/Noetic Books, 2007

The Wisdom of the Prophets (Fusus al-Hikam), Muhyi-d-din Ibn 'Arabi, Beshara Publications, 1975

Tibetan Yoga and Secret Doctrines: Or, Seven Books of Wisdom of the Great Path, according to the late Lama Kazi Dawa-Samdup's, W. Y. Evans-Wentz (Editor) , New York: Oxford University Press, 1967

Transform your energy - Change your life!, Nichiren Buddhism 3.0, Susanne Matsudo-Kiliani, Yukio Matsudo, Create Space Independent Publishing Platform, 2016

BIOGRAPHY

Professor K.A. Shakoor's immersion in an array of devotional disciplines began with a single concept. As a child, his innate sense that all creation emanates from one source began his lifelong journey to explore this truth. His experience is one of inherent faith, dedicated study and celebration of the spiritual spectrum as it is refracted through human consciousness.

EARLY YEARS

Born to a family centered on spiritual and musical enrichment, Shakoor's path was blessed early in life by his mother, Ella Ramsey Cabell, who trained him in spiritual aspects of Christianity and read the Bible to him every day; and whose own father held a Ph.D. in Theology from Columbia University. Her brother, Fred D. Ramsey as a noted mortician with whom a frequently sickly young

Shakoor spent much time discussing aspects of our impermanence, as well as practical history concerning ancient Egyptian preservation techniques (embalming) and concepts of the afterlife. The questioning and curiosity sparked at this impressionable period of his youth set the tone for a lifetime of seeking the essential truth of our nature and existence. A strong Christian influence was Reverend Carlisle Stuart, who led the nondenominational church Shakoor attended until his conversion to Sufism at thirteen. He was also impacted by the mystical and esoteric aspects of Christianity as taught by Reverend Gary Simpson of the Church of I AM. Classical organ music and vocal training occupied him through the age of seventeen. His interest in the ideas of Plato, Aristotle and other Greek philosophy sparked as early as age five, and for the next two years, he consumed books on the subject. At eight he became acquainted with Aiki and Zen Buddhist traditions and began to practice Aikido, Aiki breathing and basic Hatha yoga exercises. During his teenage years, he studied Hatha yoga at the Integral Yoga Institute founded by Sri Swami Satchidananda.

ACADEMIC YEARS

At 19 years old Shakoor earned a degree in Philosophy and Psychology from the University of Michigan-Dearborn. In Southern Michigan, during the 80's and 90's he earned professional certificates in substance abuse counseling from Wayne State University and worked in the mental health field in various capacities. I was a private student of Freudian and Jungian psychology under Professor Robert Perkins, Director of the Substance Abuse and Mental Health Department at New Center Hospital, Detroit. He also provided academic instruction of energetics and mind-body disciplines throughout the area, most notably at Wayne County Community College, Marygrove College, University of Detroit- Mercy and University of Michigan-Dearborn. As a Commander Chaplain, he also taught mind-body disciplines at the Detroit Police Academy. In 2013 Shakoor graduated from Dragon Rises College of Oriental Medicine with a Master's Degree in Oriental Medicine where he currently teaches Oriental Energy Exercises. He teaches Tai Chi Chuan, Qi-Gong, and Meditation at Santa Fe Community College and at the Karma Thegsum Choling Buddhist Meditation Center.

<u>MIND-BODY TRAINING</u>

His early teachers included Eddie Moore Sensei, Jerome Hilton Sensei in Yoshinkai Aikido, and Herman Hurst Sensei. Shakoor studied Yang Tai Chi Chuan, Hunan style Hsing-I, and Qi-Gong as a private student for seventeen years with Mr. Anton Semper, Roger Wohletz, and Master George Shu of the White Dragon Association. Master George Shu and Roger Wohletz recognized Shakoor's Maahaah-Rooh energetic mind-body system. For seven years he studied Kriya yoga, Hatha yoga, and Taoist yoga as well as Shaolin Kung Fu as a private student with Sifu Kenneth Parker, who is a direct disciple of the famous Indian Kriya yogi Shree Maharajah and direct disciple of the internationally known Kung Fu master Dennis Brown.

Shakoor spent 12 years studying Ju-Jitsu, Judo, and Baguazhan with Grand Master Seyku Bomani. He received Dan ranking under the late Professor Florendo Visitation, an internationally known martial arts innovator from New York. He studied the basics of Iaido (Japanese sword) under John Viol Sensei. He studied Aikido and Iaido under Katsumi Niikura Sensei. Shakoor studied Chen style Tai Chi, Yang style Tai Chi sword privately with Professor Nihon Yang. Shakoor studied the basics of African Martial Arts under several of Kilindi Iyi's senior students. He also spent several years as a private student of the late legendary Bey Wali in Chicago, studying the basics of Yang Tai Chi and Qi-Gong. He was a private student of Terry Burney for three years in the arts of Muay Thai kickboxing and Kriya Yoga. Shakoor also learned energetic mind-body theory under the direction of Professor Kareem Darwish, who was a senior student of Professor Milford Graves and Sifu Roosevelt Gainey of New York.

SPIRITUAL TRAINING

Buddhist Experience

Tibetan Buddhism and Buddhism have figured in Shakoor's life since he was thirteen. He received initiations and empowerments from Lamas in the Gelupa, Kagyu and Nyingma Buddhist traditions. Some of the teacher influences have been from The 16th Karmapa, Gelak Rinpoche, Lama Gyurme, Lama Dawa. In the last six years, he has been studying meditation and Buddhist teachings under Karma Kagyu Lama Losang (Dr. David Bole.)

Vedic Experience

Important to note is the prominence of matriarchal roles and maternal power in the ancient and enduring religious practices, and the powerful influence this had on Shakoor's education in regard to these religions. For seven years Shakoor studied ancient Dravidian, Kemetic and Tantric yoga under Guru A.A. Bhairava.

He was initiated into Kriya yoga under Swami Prajnananda who was a direct disciple of Swami Harihariananda and at the time the last living disciple of Swami Yukestrar, a direct student of Lahiri Mahasaya who received Kriya yoga directly from Maha Avatar Babaji. This disciplic succession, or paramparaa, is significant. According to the Bhagavad Gita (4.1) the science of yoga was delivered directly from the Supreme to the sun-god to the father of mankind. It cannot be reinterpreted, but handed down through a direct succession of disciples going back to that remote, legendary time.

Shakoor also received Kriya Tantric initiations from the late Guru Sunyata Savaswati. He was also a private student of Hurley Terrell who taught him Kundalini yoga as taught by Yogi Bhajan. He was also initiated into the Shaktipat of Swami Muktananda by Muruga Sharma.

Additionally, he taught Tai chi Chuan, Qi-Gong and Yoga for fourteen years at the International Society for Krishna Consciousness, Iskcon Temple (Fisher Mansion,) Detroit, Michigan. While there, he studied Reiki and healing sciences and became a Reiki Master under the late Parama Vismitas Haribol (Pamela Scott.) During this time he also had a very close relationship and learned directly from the late Swami Krishnapada (B.T. Swami,) who also strongly suggested that he should teach spirituality and energetics.

Sufi Experience

Shakoor's had many years of training in Sufism. His initiation into Sufism was from Muhammed Mubarak, an early teacher who began his basic education and provided a strong foundation. He spent many years in the Tijaniyya Sufic order making a pilgrimage to the tomb of Shaykh Ahmed Tijaniy (in Fez, Morocco) and meeting with the high Shaykhs there. He studied under Shaykh Haassan Cisse (based in Kaolok, Senegal) through Mahmoud Salaam and Ibrahim Muhyee Muhammed. He received two Mudlak (Master) level degrees, in Quranic and Sufi healing practices which are comparable to a Doctorate in Theology. Shakoor was initiated in the Burhaniya Shadhiliyya order under the late Shaykh Mahmoud Suliman in the Sudan. He was also initiated by three of Shaykh Ahmadu Bamba grandsons (Shaykh Ahmad Ibn Muhammad Ibn Habiballah of Senegal, 1854-1927) into the Tariqa Muriddiyah (Way of the Prophet.)

Additional Spiritual Training

Shakoor studied Torah and Old Testament with the late Rabbi Gorman, and with Rabbi Moshe in New York City. He also received basic instruction in Nkese and Yoruba traditional West African and Afro-Cuban religions under the Cuban high priest Sabu.

Over time Shakoor's efforts have cultivated a basic awareness of the truth. There is a common source back to which all human expressions of spirituality can be traced like tributaries leading back to the mighty river of their origin.

Note: *In American culture is not commonly thought that a Black skinned person can or have achieved higher levels of spiritual attainment in eastern esoteric traditions. Shakoor has studied many different traditions, and with teachers of different gender and races. In addition, it is worth mentioning that many of Shakoor's spiritual teachers mentioned above were also American Black.*

Made in the USA
San Bernardino, CA
27 September 2016